This book is for:

From:

DEAR DAUGHTER,

I've always wanted to tell you...

A LITTLE
BOOK OF
LETTERS

*E*very flower is unique: the colors, the petals, the way they dance in the breeze. But you are the most unique and beautiful of all, because:

$\mathcal{I}$'m always so, so proud of you.
Some of the things about you
that especially make me glow with
pride are:

You amaze me in countless ways. I remember one time when:

When I'm with you, these are things I feel inside:

If you were an animal, this is what I think you'd look like. (I did my best drawing it!)

$\mathcal{I}$ picked this for you because:

I love being with you. One of my favorite memories is the time we:

for ♥ YOU

*Y*ou are so funny! You made me laugh so hard when you said:

I could fill a dictionary with the remarkable words that describe you! Here are some of my favorites:

n the day you were born, I felt:

$\mathcal{I}$f I could give you an award, it would be for:

Here is a picture
of my heart.
And here is a
drawing of you
inside my heart, just
like you always are.

$\mathcal{I}$'m so glad you're my
daughter because:

If you were a book, here's what I would title it:

And my favorite chapter would be about:

$\mathcal{Y}$ ou are a masterpiece! And every color reminds me of you. Here's what each means to me:

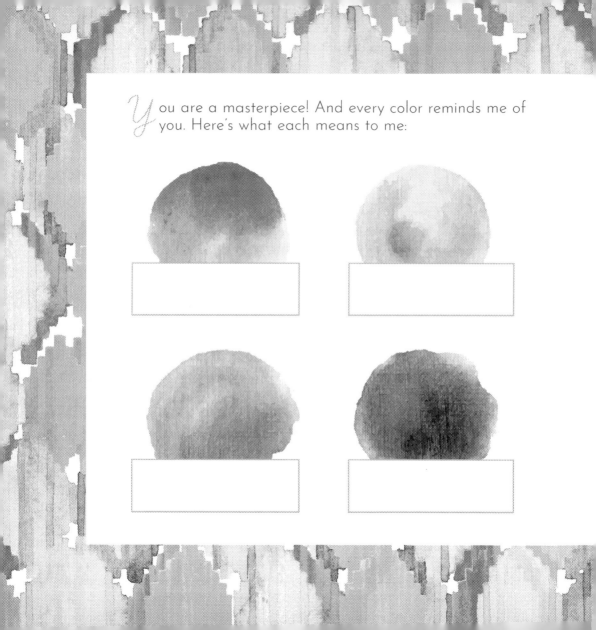

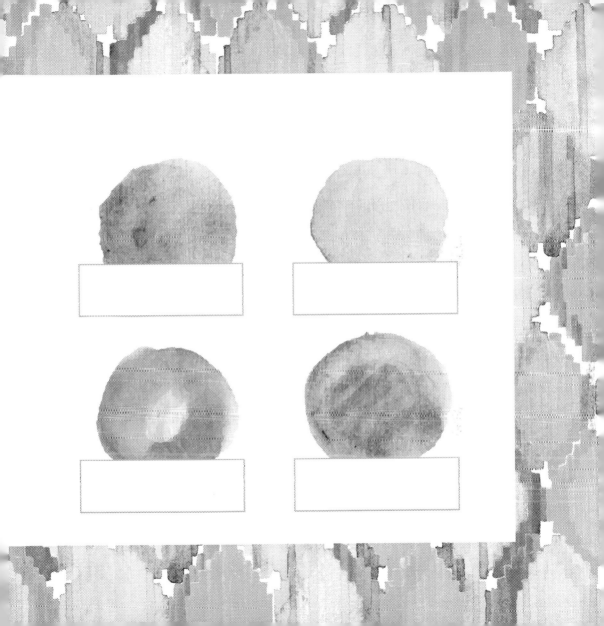

The next time you look in the mirror, I hope you can see yourself the way I do. Here is what I see in you:

Look, I drew a picture of us!

$\mathcal{Y}$ou have so many gifts to share with the world, like:

ne day, I hope:

$\mathcal{H}$ere are some of my favorite moments together.

When I wish upon a star,
here is what I wish for you:

One thing I always want
you to remember is:

Thinking
of
...YOU...

BUSHEL
& PECK
BOOKS

Bushel & Peck Books is dedicated to fighting illiteracy all over the world.
For every book we sell, we donate one to a child in need—book for book.
To nominate a school or organization to receive free books,
please visit www.bushelandpeckbooks.com.

Type set in Braisetto, Bell, and HMS Gilbert.

ISBN: 9781638190356

First Edition

Printed in the United States

10 9 8 7 6 5 4 3 2 1

BUSHEL
& PECK
BOOKS

About the Publisher

*B*ushel & Peck Books is a children's publishing house with a special mission. Through our Book-for-Book Promise™, we donate one book to kids in need for every book we sell. Our beautiful books are given to kids through schools, libraries, local neighborhoods, shelters, nonprofits, and also to many selfless organizations who are working hard to make a difference. So thank you for purchasing this book! Because of you, another book will find itself in the hands of a child who needs it most.

Printed in the United States
by Baker & Taylor Publisher Services